LISTEN TO YOUR HEART

ALSO BY MARIËLLE S. SMITH

52 Weeks of Writing Author Journal and Planner, Vol. I:
Get out of your own way and become the writer you're meant to be

52 Weeks of Writing Author Journal and Planner, Vol. II:
Get out of your own way and become the writer you're meant to be

52 Weeks of Writing Author Journal and Planner, Vol. III:
Get out of your own way and become the writer you're meant to be

99 Writing Prompts and Journal Exercises for Writers to Cultivate Courage
and Kick Imposter Syndrome to the Curb

365 Days of Gratitude Journal:
Commit to the life-changing power of gratitude by creating a sustainable practice

365 Days of Gratitude Journal, Vol. II:
Commit to the life-changing power of gratitude by creating a sustainable practice

Fleshing Out the Narrative: A 31-Day Tarot and Journal Challenge for Writers

Get Out of Your Own Way: A 31-Day Tarot Challenge for Writers and Other Creatives

Set Yourself Up for Success: A 31-Day Tarot Challenge for Writers and Other Creatives

Seven Simple Spreads 1: Seven Simple Card Spreads to Unlock Your Creative Flow

Seven Simple Spreads 2: Seven Simple Card Spreads to Direct Your Creative Flow

Seven Simple Spreads 3: Seven Simple Card Spreads to Boost Your Creative Confidence

Seven Simple Spreads 4: Seven Simple Card Spreads to Celebrate Your Creative Wins

Speak Your Truth: A 31-Day Tarot Challenge for Writers and Other Creatives

Step Into Your Power: A 31-Day Tarot Challenge to Unleash Your Creative Potential

Tarot for Creatives: 21 Tarot Spreads to (Re)Connect to Your Intuition and Ignite that Creative Spark

Tarot for Entrepreneurs: 50 Tarot Spreads and Other Intentional Practices
to Build Your Business and Tackle Its Challenges from the Heart

CO-WRITTEN UNDER THE PEN NAME HEATHER MACLEE

Too Good to Be True?

Where There's a Will

There's a Way

LISTEN TO YOUR HEART

A 31-day tarot challenge

to embrace and follow your
wildest dreams and desires

Mariëlle S. Smith

A heart will say amazing things
if it's given half a chance.

Joan Bauer

INTRODUCTION

Your heart knows what it wants. But do you?

Listen to Your Heart: A 31-Day Tarot Challenge to Embrace and Follow Your Wildest Dreams and Desires is designed to help you figure out just that.

Listen to Your Heart invites you to sit with your heart for thirty-one days to unravel:

- where you've been listening to your heart and where you haven't,
- how your heart relates to your body, mind, and soul,
- how these relationships can be improved on,
- what your heart truly wants of and for you, now and in the future, and
- the steps you must take to honour what's in your heart.

If you're ready to start listening to your heart and embrace the path it so wants to lead you towards, this tarot challenge is the perfect tool to start that conversation.

Doing a tarot challenge

If you've never done a tarot challenge before, you might wonder how it works. The answer to that is: quite simply. Each day, you pick up your deck of choice, shuffle to your heart's content, and pick one card or more, depending on the question or prompt and what your gut tells you. The next day, you put all card(s) back into your deck, shuffle like you mean it, and pull out your next draw.

During challenges, I only suggest the number of cards you could be drawing on occasion, but you are absolutely free to draw as many as you like, no matter what day or question you're on. Your gut always knows best. Likewise, it doesn't matter how you shuffle your cards or decide which card is the one that needs picking that day. Just go with what you've been taught or feels right for you in the moment. There's really no doing this wrong.

The same goes for how you interpret the cards' messages. Some cardslingers feel utterly comfortable using the guidebook that came with their deck, while others rely solely on their intuition. You can do either or a bit of both: when doing a reading, I don't mind having a glance at the description offered by the creator of the cards, especially when I feel there is more to a card than I'm able to grasp at that time. The guidebook won't always bridge that gap, but it might just give you another perspective, that 'Ah, of course!' moment that will kickstart your intuition and deepen your reading. Whatever you do, don't let others tell you what is right and wrong: there's only a right and wrong for you, and you will know what is what in the moment.

I highly suggest that you write down your findings and reflect on them as you go. The same card might show up again and again: what could that mean? Some cards will only make sense later, after you answer a few more questions. Reflecting on the cards you drew on previous days will be especially relevant in those cases. And, even if all the cards make perfect sense the moment you draw them, looking at the bigger picture after you've completed the challenge might still reveal something you hadn't considered before and bring yet another layer to what you've already unravelled.

Use whatever works for you

Those familiar with my work know that I don't differentiate between means of divination. I might use the word tarot, but you can use any kind of card deck that feels right to you when you think about this challenge. If you'd rather use your crystals or your runes, feel free to go with that.

Those who want to do the challenge but aren't comfortable using any of those divinatory tools, or simply don't own any, can even use each question as a journaling prompt.

Likewise, if you'd rather mix things up – perhaps the one question makes you want to grab your favourite oracle deck, while another makes you pick up a notebook – please do. Your challenge, your rules.

Whatever you decide on doing, I do recommend sitting down in a quiet space and taking a few deep breaths in and out to centre and ground yourself. For this challenge, I recommend four rounds or more of box breathing, but you can of course use whichever technique you're comfortable with.

Box breathing

Place one or both hands over your heart. Breathe in for four counts, hold for four counts, breathe out for four counts, and then hold again for four counts. Breathe in again for four counts, hold for four counts, breathe out for four counts, and hold for four counts. Repeat this cycle of breath two more times or until you feel ready to draw your card(s).

DAY 1

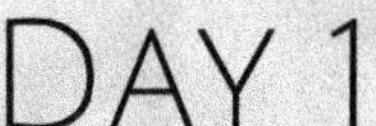

Before you shuffle your cards and ask them your question, I'd like to invite you to do the following breathing exercise to help you feel centred and grounded.

Place one or both hands over your heart. For four rounds or more, breathe in for four counts, hold for four counts, breathe out for four counts, and hold again for four counts. Once you feel centred, direct your focus to the question and draw your card(s).

———

Where's my heart at today?

DAY 2

Before you shuffle your cards and ask them your question, I'd like to invite you to do the following breathing exercise to help you feel centred and grounded.

Place one or both hands over your heart. For four rounds or more, breathe in for four counts, hold for four counts, breathe out for four counts, and hold again for four counts. Once you feel centred, direct your focus to the question and draw your card(s).

How did my heart get there?

DAY 3

Before you shuffle your cards and ask them your question, I'd like to invite you to do the following breathing exercise to help you feel centred and grounded.

Place one or both hands over your heart. For four rounds or more, breathe in for four counts, hold for four counts, breathe out for four counts, and hold again for four counts. Once you feel centred, direct your focus to the question and draw your card(s).

How is the current relationship
between my heart and my body?

DAY 4

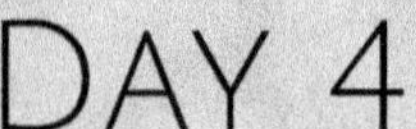

Before you shuffle your cards and ask them your question, I'd like to invite you to do the following breathing exercise to help you feel centred and grounded.

Place one or both hands over your heart. For four rounds or more, breathe in for four counts, hold for four counts, breathe out for four counts, and hold again for four counts. Once you feel centred, direct your focus to the question and draw your card(s).

How did they get there (card 1),
and what can I do to (further)
improve this relationship (card 2)?

DAY 5

Before you shuffle your cards and ask them your question, I'd like to invite you to do the following breathing exercise to help you feel centred and grounded.

Place one or both hands over your heart. For four rounds or more, breathe in for four counts, hold for four counts, breathe out for four counts, and hold again for four counts. Once you feel centred, direct your focus to the question and draw your card(s).

How is the current relationship between my heart and my head?

DAY 6

*Before you shuffle your cards and ask them your
question, I'd like to invite you to do the following
breathing exercise to help you feel centred and
grounded.*

*Place one or both hands over your heart. For four
rounds or more, breathe in for four counts, hold for
four counts, breathe out for four counts, and hold
again for four counts. Once you feel centred, direct
your focus to the question and draw your card(s).*

How did they get there (card 1),
and what can I do to (further)
improve this relationship (card 2)?

DAY 7

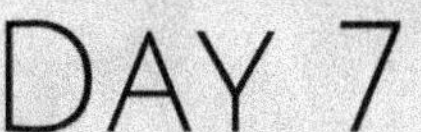

Before you shuffle your cards and ask them your question, I'd like to invite you to do the following breathing exercise to help you feel centred and grounded.

Place one or both hands over your heart. For four rounds or more, breathe in for four counts, hold for four counts, breathe out for four counts, and hold again for four counts. Once you feel centred, direct your focus to the question and draw your card(s).

How is the current relationship
between my heart and my soul?

DAY 8

Before you shuffle your cards and ask them your question, I'd like to invite you to do the following breathing exercise to help you feel centred and grounded.

Place one or both hands over your heart. For four rounds or more, breathe in for four counts, hold for four counts, breathe out for four counts, and hold again for four counts. Once you feel centred, direct your focus to the question and draw your card(s).

How did they get there (card 1),
and what can I do to (further)
improve this relationship (card 2)?

DAY 9

*Before you shuffle your cards and ask them your
question, I'd like to invite you to do the following
breathing exercise to help you feel centred and
grounded.*

*Place one or both hands over your heart. For four
rounds or more, breathe in for four counts, hold for
four counts, breathe out for four counts, and hold
again for four counts. Once you feel centred, direct
your focus to the question and draw your card(s).*

Which of my heart's dreams and
desires do I easily embrace (card 1),
and why is it so easy for me to
listen to these specifically (card 2)?

DAY 10

Before you shuffle your cards and ask them your question, I'd like to invite you to do the following breathing exercise to help you feel centred and grounded.

Place one or both hands over your heart. For four rounds or more, breathe in for four counts, hold for four counts, breathe out for four counts, and hold again for four counts. Once you feel centred, direct your focus to the question and draw your card(s).

Which of my heart's dreams and desires do I struggle to acknowledge (card 1), and why do I find it so hard to listen to these specifically (card 2)?

DAY 11

Before you shuffle your cards and ask them your question, I'd like to invite you to do the following breathing exercise to help you feel centred and grounded.

Place one or both hands over your heart. For four rounds or more, breathe in for four counts, hold for four counts, breathe out for four counts, and hold again for four counts. Once you feel centred, direct your focus to the question and draw your card(s).

Which dreams and desires have I been following that aren't my own (card 1), and why have I been listening to these specifically (card 2)?

DAY 12

Before you shuffle your cards and ask them your question, I'd like to invite you to do the following breathing exercise to help you feel centred and grounded.

Place one or both hands over your heart. For four rounds or more, breathe in for four counts, hold for four counts, breathe out for four counts, and hold again for four counts. Once you feel centred, direct your focus to the question and draw your card(s).

How has my inability to fully
listen to my own heart
affected me in the past?

DAY 13

Before you shuffle your cards and ask them your question, I'd like to invite you to do the following breathing exercise to help you feel centred and grounded.

Place one or both hands over your heart. For four rounds or more, breathe in for four counts, hold for four counts, breathe out for four counts, and hold again for four counts. Once you feel centred, direct your focus to the question and draw your card(s).

How does my inability to
fully listen to my own heart
affect me today?

DAY 14

Before you shuffle your cards and ask them your question, I'd like to invite you to do the following breathing exercise to help you feel centred and grounded.

Place one or both hands over your heart. For four rounds or more, breathe in for four counts, hold for four counts, breathe out for four counts, and hold again for four counts. Once you feel centred, direct your focus to the question and draw your card(s).

How has my listening to other people's dreams and desires instead of my own affected me in the past?

DAY 15

Before you shuffle your cards and ask them your question, I'd like to invite you to do the following breathing exercise to help you feel centred and grounded.

Place one or both hands over your heart. For four rounds or more, breathe in for four counts, hold for four counts, breathe out for four counts, and hold again for four counts. Once you feel centred, direct your focus to the question and draw your card(s).

———

How does my listening to other people's dreams and desires instead of my own affect me today?

DAY 16

Before you shuffle your cards and ask them your question, I'd like to invite you to do the following breathing exercise to help you feel centred and grounded.

Place one or both hands over your heart. For four rounds or more, breathe in for four counts, hold for four counts, breathe out for four counts, and hold again for four counts. Once you feel centred, direct your focus to the question and draw your card(s).

What does my heart want for me?

DAY 17

Before you shuffle your cards and ask them your question, I'd like to invite you to do the following breathing exercise to help you feel centred and grounded.

Place one or both hands over your heart. For four rounds or more, breathe in for four counts, hold for four counts, breathe out for four counts, and hold again for four counts. Once you feel centred, direct your focus to the question and draw your card(s).

What does my heart desire of me?

DAY 18

Before you shuffle your cards and ask them your question, I'd like to invite you to do the following breathing exercise to help you feel centred and grounded.

Place one or both hands over your heart. For four rounds or more, breathe in for four counts, hold for four counts, breathe out for four counts, and hold again for four counts. Once you feel centred, direct your focus to the question and draw your card(s).

What is currently my heart's
biggest dream or desire for me?

DAY 19

Before you shuffle your cards and ask them your question, I'd like to invite you to do the following breathing exercise to help you feel centred and grounded.

Place one or both hands over your heart. For four rounds or more, breathe in for four counts, hold for four counts, breathe out for four counts, and hold again for four counts. Once you feel centred, direct your focus to the question and draw your card(s).

What do I love about this dream or desire (card 1), and what can I do to embrace and follow it to the fullest (card 2)?

DAY 20

Before you shuffle your cards and ask them your question, I'd like to invite you to do the following breathing exercise to help you feel centred and grounded.

Place one or both hands over your heart. For four rounds or more, breathe in for four counts, hold for four counts, breathe out for four counts, and hold again for four counts. Once you feel centred, direct your focus to the question and draw your card(s).

What do I fear about this
dream or desire (card 1), and
how can I stop these fears
from stopping me (card 2)?

DAY 21

Before you shuffle your cards and ask them your question, I'd like to invite you to do the following breathing exercise to help you feel centred and grounded.

Place one or both hands over your heart. For four rounds or more, breathe in for four counts, hold for four counts, breathe out for four counts, and hold again for four counts. Once you feel centred, direct your focus to the question and draw your card(s).

What step can I take today to start honouring this dream or desire (card 1), and what does my heart want me to know about this step (card 2)?

Take the advice from your cards, then go do the thing!

DAY 22

Before you shuffle your cards and ask them your question, I'd like to invite you to do the following breathing exercise to help you feel centred and grounded.

Place one or both hands over your heart. For four rounds or more, breathe in for four counts, hold for four counts, breathe out for four counts, and hold again for four counts. Once you feel centred, direct your focus to the question and draw your card(s).

What does my heart want me to know about the step I took yesterday?

DAY 23

Before you shuffle your cards and ask them your question, I'd like to invite you to do the following breathing exercise to help you feel centred and grounded.

Place one or both hands over your heart. For four rounds or more, breathe in for four counts, hold for four counts, breathe out for four counts, and hold again for four counts. Once you feel centred, direct your focus to the question and draw your card(s).

Where will my heart lead me once I decide to fully embrace and follow my wildest dreams and desires?

DAY 24

Before you shuffle your cards and ask them your question, I'd like to invite you to do the following breathing exercise to help you feel centred and grounded.

Place one or both hands over your heart. For four rounds or more, breathe in for four counts, hold for four counts, breathe out for four counts, and hold again for four counts. Once you feel centred, direct your focus to the question and draw your card(s).

What will this path teach me about myself (card 1) and my purpose during this lifetime (card 2)?

DAY 25

Before you shuffle your cards and ask them your question, I'd like to invite you to do the following breathing exercise to help you feel centred and grounded.

Place one or both hands over your heart. For four rounds or more, breathe in for four counts, hold for four counts, breathe out for four counts, and hold again for four counts. Once you feel centred, direct your focus to the question and draw your card(s).

How do I ready myself for this journey?

DAY 26

Before you shuffle your cards and ask them your question, I'd like to invite you to do the following breathing exercise to help you feel centred and grounded.

Place one or both hands over your heart. For four rounds or more, breathe in for four counts, hold for four counts, breathe out for four counts, and hold again for four counts. Once you feel centred, direct your focus to the question and draw your card(s).

Once I'm on this path, what might try to throw me off it?

DAY 27

Before you shuffle your cards and ask them your question, I'd like to invite you to do the following breathing exercise to help you feel centred and grounded.

Place one or both hands over your heart. For four rounds or more, breathe in for four counts, hold for four counts, breathe out for four counts, and hold again for four counts. Once you feel centred, direct your focus to the question and draw your card(s).

What internal energy do I need
to invoke to stay on this path?

DAY 28

Before you shuffle your cards and ask them your question, I'd like to invite you to do the following breathing exercise to help you feel centred and grounded.

Place one or both hands over your heart. For four rounds or more, breathe in for four counts, hold for four counts, breathe out for four counts, and hold again for four counts. Once you feel centred, direct your focus to the question and draw your card(s).

What external energy do I need
to invoke to stay on this path?

DAY 29

Before you shuffle your cards and ask them your question, I'd like to invite you to do the following breathing exercise to help you feel centred and grounded.

Place one or both hands over your heart. For four rounds or more, breathe in for four counts, hold for four counts, breathe out for four counts, and hold again for four counts. Once you feel centred, direct your focus to the question and draw your card(s).

What do I know now about my heart that I didn't know before?

DAY 30

Before you shuffle your cards and ask them your question, I'd like to invite you to do the following breathing exercise to help you feel centred and grounded.

Place one or both hands over your heart. For four rounds or more, breathe in for four counts, hold for four counts, breathe out for four counts, and hold again for four counts. Once you feel centred, direct your focus to the question and draw your card(s).

What do I know now about myself (card 1) and my purpose during this lifetime (card 2) that I didn't know before?

DAY 31

Before you shuffle your cards and ask them your question, I'd like to invite you to do the following breathing exercise to help you feel centred and grounded.

Place one or both hands over your heart. For four rounds or more, breathe in for four counts, hold for four counts, breathe out for four counts, and hold again for four counts. Once you feel centred, direct your focus to the question and draw your card(s).

———

Draw one or two cards, asking: 'How do I fully embrace my heart so I can chase my wildest dreams and desires now and in the future?'

Use the card(s) you drew to create a mantra that will help you do just that.

PLEASE CONSIDER LEAVING A REVIEW

Authors are nowhere without honest reviews, and I'd truly appreciate it if you left one on Goodreads, my Facebook pages (facebook.com/thecoachforcreatives & facebook.com/mswordsmith), or the retailer where you bought this book.

THE CREATIVE CARDSLINGERS

ISN'T IT BETTER TO SLING CARDS TOGETHER?

Join my private Facebook group The Creative Cardslingers (password **RUBY ZOISITE**) to meet fellow cardreaders, be the first to test my latest card spreads, and hear all about the creative projects I'm involved in.

ABOUT ME

I'm a writer, an editor, and I coach fellow creatives on their path to fulfilling their creative calling using a combination of life coaching, Akashic Records readings, cartomancy, and Reiki. Born in the Netherlands, I moved to the island of Cyprus in February 2019.

Being somewhere new opens your mind up to other perspectives and new ideas. In my case, my spiritual side demanded to be heard more. I've always been spiritually inclined, but bringing the spiritual into my work was a scary step for me because that was not what I was known for professionally at the time. As such, I'd always tried to keep the two separate.

I say 'tried' because, even before moving to Cyprus, quite a few of my clients forced me to merge my professional background with my spiritual interests. Some hired me to edit or translate their holistic books, and others came to me for coaching and were struggling in a way that needed a broader approach.

Over the past five years, the spiritual has fully entered my workspace. This book you have in front of you right now is one of its many manifestations. It goes without saying that I hope you'll enjoy it and get from it everything you need.

If you want to get in touch with me, there
are different ways and places to do so:

mswordsmith.nl | marielle@mswordsmith.nl
instagram.com/mariellessmith
instagram.com/tarotforcreatives
facebook.com/thecoachforcreatives
facebook.com/mswordsmith

ACKNOWLEDGEMENTS

The publication of this book would not have been possible without the support of those who backed my Kickstarter campaign for the special edition of *Listen to Your Heart*.

My eternal gratitude goes out to the following people and every backer who wished to remain anonymous:

Michelle MN Jo-Anne Blanchard, Dana S, Valerie Kan, Bobbie Jean King, Linda Rodriguez, Anne Ragnhild Mandrup Christensen, Nijeara 'Ny' Buie, Clarissa, Tracy Banghart, Nicole Urbanski, Jessica Maher, Kelly Ringle, Christine M Husted, Tysha DivinationDragon, Julia Mozingo, Shannon Donbier, José Pablo Zaragoza, Stone, Keandra Johnson, Jennifer Huber, Danielle Davis, Mary Collin, Jessica Arden Cline, Alexandra Corrsin, Chain Assembly, Tisha C, Soukaïna, Viannah E. Duncan, Billy Jo Ayakatubby, Alana Nedd, Elysia V. Thorne, Alex Aeschliman, Lauren Welch, Claire McGregor, Anya Bertolet

I can't thank you enough for your support
and indulging my dreams.